BARACK OBAMA BIRTH

QUESTIONS RAISED BY DONALD TRUMP, JOE ARPAIO AND A TEA PARTY GROUP

By

Jeff Lichter

The Two Prominent Obama Questioners

PUBLICATION

A Publication of Wide Endeavors, LLC

An Arizona Corporation

By

Jeff Lichter

INTRODUCTION – FOREWORD

THIS IS THE TRUE STORY

Of how an average American motivated by the question of Barack Obama's eligibility to serve as POTUS came to pursue that eligibility with a future POTUS, Donald Trump. And later with America's Toughest Sheriff Joe Arpaio through the investigation of the Obama birth certificate issued by the White House. Following the unexpected meeting with Trump, I describe the miraculous developments of how our Surprise Arizona Tea Party group persuaded Sheriff Joe Arpaio to conduct his official law enforcement investigation. Learn how both of these great men viewed this most serious and perhaps most debated topic of the Obama presidency. Finally hear about how Trump and Arpaio are both so similar in how they treat and value people like you and me. In Trump's case, we are the "average American" and in Arpaio's case, we are "his constituents."

DEDICATION

This book is dedicated to two of my grandchildren, Tyler & Ava, to whom Donald Trump addressed his message at the end of our meeting. I would hope that they both represent the future of all Americans their age and that President Trump will succeed by MAKING AMERICA GREAT AGAIN not just for them but for everyone.

It is also dedicated to my wife, Paulette Dupon-Lichter, who makes each and every day of my life extremely pleasant and rewarding.

TABLE OF CONTENTS

CHAPTER ONE

ABOUT DONALD TRUMP

It is possible that during Barack Obama's presidency, no issue received more public discussion than the controversy over his background and birth certificate. The comments made about it by Donald Trump were widely attributed to have accelerated a very large part of that national controversy. Getting to spend even a short amount of time with Donald Trump in relation to the controversy is a distinct privilege that circumstances allowed me to have on April 8, 2011. Regardless of the topic, the chance to be with Donald Trump to discuss anything is something that anyone would treasure not because Donald Trump is a billionaire businessman or because he delivered the biggest upset in American history to become the President of the United States almost six years later.   It is because such a hugely successful man makes you, the average American, feel very comfortable, relaxed, and even important while you are with him. He does not look down upon you as most extremely famous people do, at least subconsciously, when they happen to be with common folk. Instead, he relates to you as one human being to another, simply as one American talking to another American on equal terms. He actually attentively listens to you giving his full attention. In their book, "Let Trump Be Trump," Corey Lewandowski and David Bossie write the following about Trump. "There is so much hate and misunderstanding that people rarely get the chance to see the man for who he is. And we consider ourselves lucky." And I certainly consider myself both lucky and very fortunate.

My once in a lifetime opportunity to meet and converse with Donald Trump on that date happened as a result of an effort I had been part of to pass a law in the Arizona Legislature at the time. Along with legislators Judy Burgess, Carl Seel, and Kelly Townsend, together we had been moving legislation through the Arizona House and Senate to insure that candidates for the Presidency of the United States were properly vetted through the Secretary of States, as to their status and qualifications as a natural born citizen as required by Article II, Section I, Paragraph 5 of the United States Constitution prior to being placed on their state ballots.

CHAPTER TWO

SURPRISE ARIZONA TEA PARTY AND ELIGIBILITY LEGISLATION

The impetus for this legislation began with the Surprise Arizona Tea Party (SATP), a group that was formed by my dear friends Jim and Julie Wise, following their departure from a prior tea party group. I also left the prior group to join and develop the new SATP with them. The founding principles of the new SATP group centered around the same goals of the national Tea Party Patriots, which were limited government, financial responsibility, and free markets. While maintaining these principles as the pillars symbolizing the Tea Party purposes, our group also became extremely concerned about the complex and largely unknown facts surrounding the new Presidents eligibility for the office, or the lack thereof. We were well aware of the claims coming from so many different eligibility activists around the country including such as Phillip Berg, Dr. Orly Taitz and very many others. At the same time, we also were tuned into the many eligibility lawsuits being filed in so many jurisdictions within the country and also what was occurring with Army Lt. Col. Terry Lakin and the questions he was asking prior to being court martialled in relation to the issue. Lakin's story is told in his book " Officer's Oath". The SATP was the only group reported to have organized a demonstration rally in defense of Lt. Col. Lakin. Over fifty of our members gathered together on December 6, 2010 to demonstrate at the major intersection in Phoenix of 24th Street and Camelback Road and also petition at the offices of Senators Jon Kyl and John McCain as well as the office of Congressman Trent Franks.

Being consumed by the exploding issue of eligibility, Jim Wise and I quickly launched a major effort to institute a bill on Presidential Eligibility into the Arizona State Legislature beginning in January 2010. Jim Wise and I began that effort with a meeting with our state representative, Judy Burgess. We explained and discussed the importance of enforcing the Article II, Section 1 natural born citizen clause of the U.S. Constitution and that there was an ongoing nationwide avalanche questioning whether Barack Obama met that foundational test. Representative Burgess, added to her reputation of being a great legislator and patriot, by agreeing to sponsor the bill requiring that the Arizona Secretary of State properly vet the legitimacy of presidential

Candidates to meet the natural born citizen requirement, including but not limited to submitting a valid birth certificate.

Sarcastically labelled the "birther bill" by the media, the legislation managed to pass the House of Representatives in 2010 but was successfully politically stalled and never put to a vote in the State Senate. In spite of being killed in this manner, the bill was reintroduced by Representative Burges in January of 2011. Initially, surprisingly defeated by a very narrow vote in committee, as sponsors of the bill, we thought it was already dead. However, Representative Carl Seel allowed Judy Burgess to attach it to one of his defeated bills in what is known as a "striker bill". And then something miraculous happened.

CHAPTER THREE

A DETOUR TO TRUMP TOWER DURING THE LEGISLATION

Unbeknown to myself or fellow Tea Party activist Kelly Townsend, Representative Seel made a phone call to Trump Tower and as luck would have it got connected to Trumps attorney, Michael Cohen. It is noteworthy that this occurred during the same week that Trump was igniting the media on fire by going public daily about Obama possibly not being born in the United States. Seel informed Cohen about the eligibility bill now revived in the Arizona Legislature and Cohen responded with an invitation to Trump Tower in order to discuss it. The opportunity was more than welcomed and on April 8, 2011, Seel, Townsend, and I departed for New York

The flight itself found the three of us involved in several discussions anticipating what might happen in our meeting and trying to prepare ourselves for the many possible scenarios. It was also apparent to us that while we were eagerly anticipating the meeting, we were at the same time in a certain fear of the unknown by being with such a famous businessman who was also rumored at the time to be thinking about running for President of the United States. We wondered how he would treat and relate to just three "very common Americans" who were coming to see and talk with him. Upon arrival in New York, we departed for the night to our pre-arranged destinations. Carl and Kelly stayed at a midtown hotel and I had arranged to spend the night at my nephew's apartment on Manhattan's east side about seven or eight blocks from Trump Tower.

The next morning, we had arranged to meet an hour before the meeting time to further prepare and try to alleviate our obvious nervousness. Although we all felt this anxiety, I remember how deep my own fear of getting "paralysis of the tongue" was in my mind. I kept thinking over and over again about how I might contribute to the conversation and what I might and would say.

We decided that we had sufficient time to find a nearby church and actually go inside to pray about it and ask for God's help that the meeting would go well and be productive. If I remember correctly, I think we had to go three places of worship before we found one that would actually allow us to actually enter this early in the morning to go into an area of prayer.

CHAPTER FOUR

PRE MEETING WITH TRUMP'S ATTORNEY MICHAEL COHEN

Prayers now ended, it was time to walk the few blocks back to Trump Tower and perform. We were met in the lobby at the front of the elevator that goes to the 26th floor office of Mr. Trump by his personal attorney Michael Cohen, who was the one who had invited us when Carl Seel had reached him on the phone.

Upon reaching the 26th floor offices, Mr. Cohen escorted us into the same conference room used for the Celebrity Apprentice show where we spent about 15 minutes just speaking with him before proceeding to Donald Trump's office. Cohen spent the time speaking about his relationship with and duties for Trump and his sincere belief that Trump would actually announce his run for POTUS soon (which he did not end up doing in 2012).

He also spoke about his own family lineage and in particular his father. In regard to his dad, Cohen spoke with pride about all the time and effort it took for his father to become a U.S. citizen. Since it was my hope that the subject of natural born citizenship would come up in the next meeting with Trump, this gave me the perfect opportunity to ask and find out that Cohen had been born prior to his dad obtaining the citizenship. We then continued to have a brief conversation about natural born citizenship and Cohen acknowledged that he would not qualify as one because of his father not being a citizen at the time he was born. He added that he had no problem being prohibited from presidential eligibility because of that.

I mention this because although it was great that Mr. Trump was so focused at the time on his opinion that Obama was not born in our country, he was not addressing the even larger constitutional requirement of natural born citizenship, which would certainly have enhanced the effort he and so much of the country was engaged in over the issue.

Michael Cohen then accompanied us into Trump's office and remained throughout the meeting.

CHAPTER FIVE

HIGHLIGHTS OF THE MEETING WITH TRUMP

It would be an understatement to say that the meeting was inundated with highlights. To cite just some of them, they include Trump being deeply focused on the story from "Grandma Sarah" in Kenya, who was recorded on tape stating that she was in the hospital in Kenya and saw the birth.

We also discussed the fact that James Orengo, the Minister of Lands and a member of the Kenyan Parliament on March 25, 2010, stated to the Parliament "how could a young man born here in Kenya, and not even a native American, become President of America?"

Additionally, there was discussion about the fake Connecticut Social Security number that the President was widely being reported to be using, including on his tax return.

And then during a slight pause in the discussion, I took my chance to switch the conversation from these matters, including the actual place of birth to the encompassing and larger question of constitutional eligibility. I brought up the natural born citizen requirement in Article II, Section I, pp 5 of the Constitution and Mr. Trump asked me to explain it further.

I was not sure whether Mr. Trump was familiar with the constitutional meaning of the term, or its sources, or whether he was in effect just testing me as to my own knowledge of it. So I went ahead and quickly explained its origination in the treatise known as Vattel's Law of Nations, the study of that by the founding fathers and its roots and relationship to national security. Mr. Trump responded by stating that he very much liked my explanation and asked me to mail him documentation on it, which I did upon returning home.

The letter and the more detailed explanation of natural born citizenship that I sent to him soon after returning home is attached in the Appendix herein.

Also, it is important to point out that in this meeting, never once did any of the five participants mention a word about race, either Obama's or racial issues in America.

CHAPTER SIX

ANOTHER MEETING HIGHLIGHT – IT'S EFFECT UPON THE ARIZONA LEGISLATION

Another highlight was that Donald Trump gave us permission to inform the Arizona Legislature that he was in support of the bill before them to insure a President's eligibility by having the Secretary of State fully investigate the natural born citizen status before placing a presidential candidate on the state ballot.

Trump's endorsement of the natural born citizen legislation greatly influenced the course of our legislation and the members of the Arizona State House and Senate. Many of them were awestruck by the invitation to Trump Tower that we had received. The publicity that the trip received from the press helped to trigger a boatload of questions from the legislators when we returned.

The Legislature, both the Arizona House and Senate, went on just one week later to pass the bill on April 15, 2011 on a full party line vote, with the Republican majority unanimously voting for it. The Democrats of course wanted no part of this legislation.

Stunningly just three days later on April 18th, the Republican governor Jan Brewer, immediately vetoed the bill. Governor Brewer issued some confusing, vague, and illogical reasons for defying her entire party at the time. Many years later, when I had the opportunity to ask her directly why she vetoed it, she issued an entirely different explanation saying she was just convinced by what she was being told by the State of Hawaii. She was clearly not informed about all the obstruction, contradictions, and misinformation that was coming from the Hawaii Department of Health and continued even following her veto.

The real reasons she vetoed the bill are admittedly speculation but probably more likely related to incredible pressure she was probably receiving from not only the Obama administration, but also those such as Senator John McCain. Such pressure could be attributed to the fact that at least five other states were debating similar legislation to Arizona's at the time and the vision of more than one state passing such legislation could likely sink the President and certainly a second term.

CHAPTER SEVEN

MOST MEMORABLE HIGHLIGHT OF THE MEETING

Returning once more to the meeting in Trump Tower, the most memorable discussion was clearly when the subject of internet rumors that a fake birth certificate was forthcoming was raised. Mr. Trump commented, and I remember his words not only clearly but word for word many years later, *"yes my sources in DC are telling me that there is going to be a fake one issued soon."* Nineteen (19) days later, on April 27, 2011, Barack Obama in a nationally televised address issued for the first time what he purported to be his long form birth certificate. What happened to this birth certificate following its issuance on this date will be much further described in the next section dealing with Sheriff Joe Arpaio of Maricopa County, Arizona.

Before ending the approximately 30 minute meeting, Mr. Trump graciously offered to sign autographs and take photos with the three of us. The photo illustrated in this article shows me standing behind Mr. Trump at his desk while he signed the back of his business card for me. He asked, "who do you want me to address it to? I replied and asked him to write it to my grandchildren Tyler and Ava. He then wrote to them that "you have a great grandfather." I must admit that for him to write that about me sent chills through me and that moment and inscription will remain with me forever. I held that business card for many months thereafter debating in my mind as to whether to keep it or give it to Tyler and Ava to keep. I subsequently decided that since it was written to them that they should have it. That unfortunately turned out to be a huge mistake because being only 14 and 11 years old at the time, apparently neither was as impressed as I was or could possibly know that he would become the President of the country in 2016. The preceding is their (or mine?) excuse for the sad fact that the valuable keepsake can no longer be found today.

Trump Signs His Business Card to Tyler & Ave writing "You have a great grandfather."

Upon saying goodbye and expressing our heartfelt thanks for the meeting, we descended down the 26 floors from Trump's office to the lobby. Upon opening the elevator doors, we unexpectedly and immediately saw a long line of reporters waiting for interviews about the substance of the meeting. We had no idea who had notified the press, but Carl Seel eagerly took the opportunity to inform them and the videotape of his recorded interview was played over the next couple of days on most, if not all, of the local Phoenix TV stations.

Among those standing in the lobby with the press corps was a woman waving frantically at us. When I acknowledged her attempts to get our attention, it turned out to be a woman named Theresa Cao, who had shortly before had a televised public outburst during a hearing at the U.S. Capital chambers, during which each House member read different passages from the U.S. Constitution. This tribute to the Constitution was televised on all major cable channels. But when Representative Frank Pallone of New Jersey had his turn to read the Article II, Section I passage on the Presidential eligibility clause requiring natural born citizenship, Cao screamed out from the gallery something to the effect that Barack Obama was not one. She was immediately arrested but then released on her own recognizance pending a later day in court. Before heading to the airport to return to Phoenix, we invited Theresa to join us for lunch and discussed her obvious passion that a United States President must qualify as a natural born citizen. Of course, we let her know that the subject was discussed with both Michael Cohen and Donald Trump in both the meetings that we had.

Over the next day or two, I also let all the other many concerned American patriots that I had previously been in touch with in the year or so prior that we had discussed the natural born citizenship of Barack Obama, or lack thereof, in the meeting. Nothing of consequence has been done since to clear up the many differences of legal interpretations of the Article II, Section I, Paragraph 5 clause that exists. Some of these varied interpretations are strategically and politically motivated in order to deliberately cloud a true and certain definition. Almost everyone, including us, who asserted that Barack Obama was not a natural born citizen did so based upon the definitions provided in Vattel's Law of Nations that one had to be born of citizen parents on the soil.

The main highlight of the meeting, that of Donald Trump's comment about the fake birth certificate he had heard would be issued soon will be much further addressed in the following chapters where I speak about the times I have been fortunate to spend with Sheriff Joe Arpaio and the very courageous actions that he took and did about the issue.

CHAPTER EIGHT

ABOUT JOE ARPAIO

Sheriff Joe Arpaio is the courageous public official, and the only one, who "took the ball" from Donald Trump and the Surprise Arizona Tea Party to pursue the issue being discussed throughout the country. Known as America's Toughest Sheriff, he may be the most mis-characterized public figure in the United States as his character if so often misrepresented even as much or more than Donald Trump's has been misrepresented to the general public.

When you get to know him, it is apparent how caring he is to and for the thousands of citizens he has met through his many years as the Sheriff of Maricopa County, Arizona. In addition to his service and dedication to his constituents, his love for animals is also well known through his several prosecutions of those who have abused animals. I originally got to meet him through his many evening speaking appearances he appeared for at the Surprise Arizona Tea Party (SATP). Any and every time that the SATP invited him, he willingly accepted. He not only gave up his personal time for our group, but did so for practically each and every similar group, of which there were hundreds, throughout the Phoenix area. The Sheriff would actually point this out during most of these local speeches saying something to the effect that he was well aware of his responsibility to those who elected him and that in fact, he thought that his record of being continually re-elected could be attributed to these frequent appearances before so many different organizations and constituents. During these unprepared and informal speeches, more like just "talks", Sheriff Joe showed those in attendance how funny, honest, and politically incorrect he was. Audiences loved him for all of it. And those, like myself, who got to see and hear him numerous times realized how often he was devoting his time to us while sacrificing time he could be at home with his lovely wife Ava

CHAPTER NINE

BACK TO THE BARACK OBAMA BIRTH CERTIFICATE OF APRIL 27, 2011 ON WHITEHOUSE.GOV

First, the most obvious reason that the long form birth certificate was issued at all was because there was a national wave of continual pressure in the country for it to be released beginning at the time of Obama first becoming a candidate.

Obama very often ignored or joked about the calls for its release since then and even after his election. However, the issue continued to be written about in blog articles and the many newspapers throughout the country. It was discussed on major network and cable television channels repeatedly. And of course, it was debated vigorously in the public mostly on social media.

However, the heaviest and most weighty pressure came from both Dr. Jerome Corsi's book "Where's The Birth Certificate," and Donald Trump's repeated statements about the issue. Corsi's book was published in early 2011 and Trump's everyday narrative in the news, during April 2011 questioning the real birthplace became just too much and produced the submission on Barack Obama's part to agree to release a long form birth certificate, which he did in a televised news conference on April 27, 2011.

It must be pointed out that this release came during the same time period when the SATP was pushing the eligibility legislation in the Arizona Legislature and during which we met with Trump. Second, immediately upon its release numerous graphic experts, and even several high school "techies", found it to contain so many anomalies that they started declaring it a forgery in one way or another. These claims of a forged document exponentially multiplied to such an avalanche that it resulted in the Surprise Arizona Tea Party (SATP) successfully persuading Maricopa County AZ. Sheriff Joe Arpaio to form a Cold Case Posse (CCP) to investigate it, the origin of is much further described further in Chapter Ten.

THE BIRTH OF A LAW ENFORCEMENT INVESTIGATION BY SHERIFF JOE ARPAIO'S COLD CASE POSSE

The story behind the formation of the CCP began with a speaker appearance of Dr. Jerome Corsi at a Surprise Tea Party meeting held on August 17, 2011 just short of four months after the Obama birth certificate was issued to the public in April. Dr. Corsi came with and made available copies of his just released book entitled "Where's The Real Birth Certificate" to the large crowd. He also brought along his three to four inch thick bound collection entitled, "Eligibility," which contained the testimony that he had collected from over twenty prominent graphic researchers listing all of the varied and also overlapping reasons they all went public in writing to pronounce the birth certificate of April 27th to be a forged document. Part of the plan that evening was to collect petition signatures from the attendees to request a meeting with Maricopa County Sheriff Joe Arpaio in order to present the signatures and lobby for an investigation from law enforcement. Over 250 signatures were on the petitions gathered that night. The other part of the plan had already been implemented, that being to have the meeting pre-arranged. Therefore, the very next day, Aug. 18th, 2011 Dr. Corsi along with five members of the SATP, including myself presented the petitions and the case to the Sheriff and his staff.

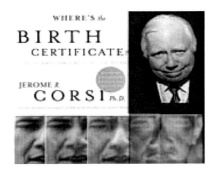

The Corsi Book

Corsi, Arpaio, Jim & Julie Wise, Jeff Lichter

During the meeting, it appeared as if our petitions and our arguments would fail because the legal and communications staff that the Sheriff called into the meeting clearly stated their objection to our effort. However, Sheriff Joe continued the discourse and continued asking questions to us. The meeting ended without an immediate decision but the very brave and extremely welcomed decision made afterwards proved how responsive he was to the concerns of his constituents.

After Sheriff Arpaio, days later announced that he had decided to form the Cold Case Posse to start the investigation that was requested; he was repeatedly questioned and criticized by the media as to why he was doing this. Being the very courageous, principled, and truthful man he is, his unequivocal and paraphrased response was always, "what am I supposed to do with the petitions from this many constituents just throw them in the basket?"

CHAPTER ELEVEN

RESULTS OF THE INVESTIGATION ANNOUNCED IN THREE PRESS CONFERENCES

Six months later on March 1, 2012,, in the first of three press conferences on the subject, the results of the Cold Case Posse investigation were announced. Lead investigator Mike Zullo and Sheriff Joe Arpaio stunned the assembled crowd of local activists and the local press in attendance by proclaiming how and why they reached their finding that there "was probable cause that the Obama birth certificate and selective service registrations were forged computer created documents." The local press was blatantly hostile throughout the conference, displaying their apathy by not taking notes, apparent facial movements indicating opposition, and then by asking the most irrelevant questions and making many combative comments during the question and answer session. On the whole, they were clearly pre-disposed to defend the Obama birth certificate regardless of the evidence presented and to oppose anything claimed, or even proved by Sheriff Arpaio, whose personality and immigration policies they had been denigrating for many years.

The evidence presented by Arpaio and Zullo included video graphics which demonstrated the Adobe Illustrator software, and how that software was used to create the document and the many "layers" it contained to be created by the White House and posted on whitehouse.gov. The videos demonstrated amongst other findings that the paper used could not have come from an original copy of a real birth certificate, and even how the official seal and stamp was moved onto the document and therefore could not have come from an original certificate, which could never be moved around on a subsequent computer program. In addition, the forged elements on the selective service registration were even more nefarious and apparent in its creation. In spite of all the detailed and clear evidence presented during the very long over one hour press conference, the media did not ask one single question about the evidence solidifying the obvious that they had their ears deliberately closed. Every one of their questions and comments addressed only subjects like Arpaio's motivations for doing this and Zullo's background as a cop in New Jersey. The full one hour and 20 minute press conference can still be seen by a google You Tube search for the Arpaio and Zullo March 1, 2012 Cold Case Posse Press Conference.

The second Press Conference was held on July 17, 2012 during which Arpaio and Zullo removed the "probable cause" label from their previous announcement and declared during the Sheriff's opening statement that "as we suspected, the birth certificate released by the White House is a fraudulent document." Arpaio also reiterated that the Obama selective service form was also fraudulent. Mike Zullo then proceeded to describe the stonewalling he received during his trip to Hawaii from officials there, clarifications to some of the findings released during the preceding press conference in March, and the new findings discovered since then, including his and World Net Daily's telephone interview with local registrar, 95 year old Verna K. Lee. This, along with additional information about the many Hawaii Health Department irregularities can be found at http://www.wnd.com/2012/07/secret-of-obamas-phantom-numbers-uncovered/. The entire event can again be seen on

You Tube by a google or you tube search for Arpaio-Zullo Cold Case Posse 2nd Press Conference of 7-17-12.

The third and final conclusive Press Conference occurred on Dec. 15, 2016 just before Sheriff Arpaio's final term in office was to end. During this event, the video evidence presented clearly demonstrated how the specific birth certificate of Johanna Ahnee, originally obtained by Jerome Corsi, was the source document for the transfer of information to the Obama created birth certificate. Identical special distances and alignments both vertically and horizontally were clearly shown to exist between the two documents. Since documents issued in Hawaii during the 1960's were all stamped by hand, this was shown and verified to be a mathematical impossibility by the forensic investigative firms both in the United States and in Italy. Both of these investigative teams did separate investigations of the White House birth certificate issued on 4-27-11 and neither knew of the others investigation. Both firms are renowned to be the best forensic document investigators in the world and both endorsed Arpaio's Cold Case Posse findings as completely valid.

The fact that the Cold Case Posse findings, publicly announced in the three press conferences were deliberately and strategically suppressed by almost all major media and cable stations just solidifies the well- known fact that the media remained fully committed to maintaining their collaboration with and marketing of the false White House narrative. The findings of the Arpaio-Zullo investigation were fully endorsed by two independent expert independent global firms as announced during the 3rd press conference. Still, it has not resulted in the repeatedly requested Congressional investigation. Congress and the media remain intimidated and paralyzed over this issue as it has been since its original arrival when Barack Obama announced his run for the presidency.

Cold Case Posse Investigation

Chief Investigator Mike Zullo Presenting Evidence

CHAPTER TWELVE

SURPRISE TEA PARTY CONTINUES PROMOTING INVESTIGATION AND THE SHERIFF

The Surprise Tea Party did not stop their pursuit of the truth with the Cold Case Posse investigation of the birth certificate. Within the several years that the investigation required, the SATP also planned additional events to promote the Cold Case Posse findings. On March 31, 2012, shortly after the first press conference, the Surprise Tea Party successfully promoted and held a special event at the Church on the Green in Sun City West Arizona which produced one of the largest Tea Party audiences recorded anywhere, an audience of 1200 persons. This audience consisted of Maricopa County residents and even many from California and other nearby states who had heard of the Arpaio Cold Case Posse Press Conference and wanted to hear this subsequent summary of it held by Sheriff Arpaio, chief investigator Mike Zullo and the Surprise Tea Party. I was heavily involved in planning this event and had the distinct honor of introducing Sheriff Joe to the very large audience.

1200 Persons at the Church on the Green

Introducing the Sheriff

Based upon the success of the Church on the Green event, the SATP planned, but failed to stage an even larger event at the Celebrity Theatre in Phoenix, which contained over 2000 seats. Whereas there was no admission charged to the event at the church, the theatre had to be rented requiring admission to be charged. To fully highlight Sheriff Arpaio's and the investigations outcry for a full congressional investigation, several prominent speakers had agreed to attend at their own expense and address the crowd. Speakers included were Joe Arpaio, Terry Lakin, Mike Zullo, Tom Ballantyne and Pat Boone, who had agreed to sing in addition to speaking on the issue. Sadly, insufficient ticket sales to cover the rent and overhead costs resulted in cancellation.

CHAPTER THIRTEEN

THE HOSPITAL VISIT

On the more personal side of my relationship with Sheriff
Joe, I must include the surprise visit he made to me on
November 18, 2014 at the Kindred Hospital in Peoria Az.
Along with Kelly Townsend and Mike Zullo, the Sheriff
suddenly appeared in my room just days after I had come
out of a coma I had been in since open heart surgery on
October 5th of that year. I had undergone a four way bypass
and had two valves replaced during a scheduled five hour
surgery that evolved into eleven hours as a result of life
threatening complications. Upon being sent to ICU when
surgery finally ended, the surgeons advised that my entire
family be told to say goodbye to me. With divine help and
my family's refusal to pull the plug, I managed to slowly
recover day by day after awakening from the coma.

And that's when Sheriff Joe appeared to bestow upon me
the everlasting honor that he took time from his busy day to
spend time over my hospital bed even when I still couldn't
really speak due to a tracheotomy (see figure 2 below). I
remember trying to smile and attempting to speak back to
him even though I also remember not knowing whether I
was dreaming or not and that he was actually there to greet
and wish me well. I also must cite the ironic fallout that
occurred after his departure. The word of the Sheriff's
appearance at Kindred spread and created quite a stir
throughout the entire hospital because over that day and the
one after, it seemed that every nurse and many doctors
peeked in and asked me if I was the patient he had visited.
Some of them were even courteous enough to ask how I
was doing!

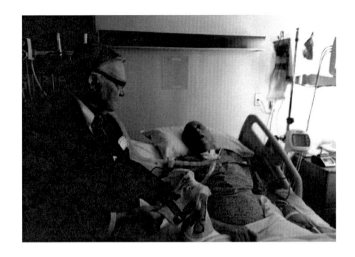

Sheriff joking about pink underwear during the visit.

CHAPTER FOURTEEN

OTHER SURPRISE TEA PARTY EVENTS

There were other events which occurred with and for the great Sheriff of Maricopa County that also deserve short mention. This would include the time in the spring of 2013 that Jim Wise and I with the backing of the SATP and well known attorney Larry Klayman served as plaintiffs in a Maricopa County lawsuit against the group led by Randy Parraz, president of Citizens for Better Arizona, which had initiated the countywide recall effort against Sheriff Joe. The suit we brought against them for violating an Arizona state statute which contained time limits for initiating a recall following a certified election severely hampered the fund raising efforts of Parraz and he failed to acquire the necessary amount of recall petitions resulting in the failure of the effort.

Other SATP events that were conducted for Sheriff Joe included the one on June 4, 2013 to celebrate the defeat of the Recall effort. We held a Meet and Greet event attended by about 150 supporters. Besides the food and drink was supplied to all and other supporters were Skyped into the room to congratulate the Sheriff for not only the defeat of the recall but for his many other accomplishments. Those who were Skyped in for a short statement included Larry Klayman, Pat Boone and Terry Lakin.

Another was on September 20, 2016 almost two years after recovering from my heart attack, the SATP invited me to present a PowerPoint full Timeline of Eligibility Events to another large

Presenting Timeline of Obama Eligibility Events

crowd of Arpaio supporters. Upon finishing the timeline (photo above), I again had the privilege of introducing the Sheriff, who proceeded to deliver the main address for the evening, again producing the stellar and humorous speech he was noted for.

CHAPTER FIFTEEN

CONCLUSION

Between them, Donald Trump highlighted and Joe Arpaio investigated one of the most, if not the pre-eminent issue of Barack Obama's presidency. Together they asked the questions that were on the minds of a many millions of Americans and so often discussed by reluctant politicians, journalists, media personalities, and in all of the social media outlets. Who was Barack Obama? Was he constitutionally eligible to become the POTUS as a natural born citizen? Was he born on U.S. soil, in Hawaii, as he claimed but couldn't verify by an original birth certificate or from a Hawaii hospital verifying such a birth? Why, on April 27, 2011 did he finally issue a birth certificate that so many pronounced as not only suspicious, but fake? Sheriff Arpaio's investigation pronounced and proved that it was a fake. Why has the Congress so far refused to investigate the birth certificate and Arpaio's findings for itself?

The last question is perhaps the most important. We must do whatever possible to receive the real answers by making Congress do their job as Sheriff Joe has repeatedly requested.

APPENDIX

1) APRIL 18, 2011 LETTER TO DONALD TRUMP

2) ENCLOSURE RE: NATURAL BORN CITIZEN

Jeff Lichter
16571 W. Stock Tr.
Surprise, AZ 85387
(623) 825-0715

April 18, 2011

Mr. Donald Trump, Chairman & President
c/o Mr. Michael D. Cohen, Exec. Vice President
The Trump Organization
725 Fifth Avenue
New York, N.Y. 10022

Subject: Natural Born Citizenship and Documented Evidence from Kenyan National Assembly

Dear Mr. Trump:

During our meeting on April 8, 2011 in your office, you asked that I send you some documented backup and additional information on two matters which were discussed in the meeting.

Accordingly, enclosed for your review, is a brief bullet point analysis of the Article II, Section I clause on NATURAL BORN CITIZENSHIP. It was deliberately kept brief as we are aware that you have received much additional and more detailed information on this from several others. We are hoping that you will decide to expand the focus from just the questionable place of birth of Mr. Obama to the question as to whether regardless of where he was born, is he constitutionally qualified as a natural born citizen?

Second, I have enclosed the documented backup highlighting the statement made on March 25, 2010 in the Kenyan National Assembly by James Orengo, the Minister of Lands, which can be found on page 31 of the Official Report from the Assembly meeting that day. Also included is an article from the Nigerian Tribune, which is typical of many articles from several different African newspapers that can be found on the Internet. And if you go to http://atlahmedianetwork/?p=1615 a tape very similar to the Grandmother recording can be found of the Kenyan Ambassador on the Mike and Mike show out of Detroit also saying that Mr. Obama was born in Kenya.

I hope this information will be helpful to you in your ongoing research of this matter.
Also, I apologize for the slight delay in responding to your request as I was fully engaged last week at the Arizona Legislature in our attempt to pass the Presidential Eligibility Legislation HB2177 sponsored by Mr. Seel which we succeeded in doing by an unexpected unanimous vote of all Republicans in both the Senate and House. Thank you for the opportunity to be of assistance.

Sincerely yours,

Jeff Lichter

Submitted by Jeff Lichter
April 18, 2011

A SIMPLE READING AND INTERPRETATION OF ARTICLE II, SECTION I CLAUSE 5 OF THE UNITED STATES CONSTITUTION

Note: Outlined in Black and Red = the primary clause
Outlined in Blue = the grandfather clause.

No person except a natural born citizen, or a citizen of the United States, at the time of the adoption of the Constitution, shall be eligible to the Office of President.

Analysis of the Sentence

1. Because the clause uses two different terms that of natural born citizen and citizen in the same sentence, it clearly means that the founders intended two different meanings for those terms.

2. Since there are two different meanings and because of the grandfather clause, it is very clear that the natural born citizen is the more restrictive of the two terms requiring that a higher standard be met than just being a citizen.

3. It is clear that the grandfather clause in blue allows the founders themselves, or citizens at the time of the adoption of the Constitution, to be President but that after they are gone, eligibility for the Presidency required a natural born citizen. No longer would plain citizens be allowed.

4. Therefore, just being born in the United States may make you a citizen but **NOT** necessarily a natural born citizen. The founders (i.e., Washington, Franklin et al) WERE born in the United States which made them citizens. But if they intended to permit just citizens to FOREVER BE ELIGIBLE, THEN THERE WOULD HAVE BEEN NO NEED FOR THE GRANDFATHER CLAUSE or use of the term natural born citizen. The clause would then have just stated simply that any citizen born in the United States was eligible.

5. The four clear conclusions above elicits the question that since eligibility now requires the higher status of being a natural born citizen, not just a citizen, what is a natural born citizen?

6. The founders knew that they themselves were British subjects and included the grandfather clause only because someone had to be eligible as President until the next generation arrived. Since the country was first being established, and all citizens were therefore still British subjects, it would obviously take another generation of citizens born of citizens to have persons who were not subjects of another country.

1

7. So again, it is clear from interpreting just Article II, Section I, Clause 5 that the difference between a citizen and a natural born citizen had to do with requiring parental lineage to citizens who had no allegiances to other countries.

8. We know the founders were students of Vattel's Law of Nations particularly Book I, Chapter 19, Section 212 which defined natural born citizens as those born on the soil to citizen parents or at the very least to a citizen father. Also, Article I, Section 8 of the US Constitution contains a clause giving Congress the power to enforce any and all offenses against the Law of Nations.

9. Anyone who disagrees with the definition or distinction above between citizen and natural born citizen would then have the burden of providing their own documented definition of what constitutes a natural born citizen. That alternative definition would have to avoid being the equivalent of what a plain citizen is and would have to demonstrate an alternative meaning that still constituted a higher standard over the plain citizen. It has not and cannot be done.

Note: Much more information on Natural Born Citizenship and Vattel's Law of Nations can be found at www.puzo1.blogspot.com, written by Mario Apuzzo, Esq.

Made in United States
North Haven, CT
05 June 2022

19873147R00027